IF'S AND'S OR BUTTS & GUTS

AN INTRIGUING INSIDE LOOK AT CREATING OPTIMAL HEALTH AND QUALITY OF LIFE THROUGH NUTRITION

Nicki

To Your internal and eternal Health and Wellness.

Love,
Dr Becky

BY

BECKY NATRAJAN, M.D.

IF'S AND'S OR BUTTS
AND GUTS

COPYRIGHT © 2005 BY BECKY NATRAJAN, M.D.

BECKY NATRAJAN M.D. AND DAN MAES
QUALITY OF LIFE INTERNATIONAL
4351 E. PINNACLE RIDGE PL.
TUCSON, AZ 85718
(520) 529-7479
DMAES@COMCAST.NET

ISBN: 0-9771130-0

First Edition
Printed in the United States of America

Contents

Foreword ───────────────────

By Dan Maes

Every morning when the doctor approached her patient's bedside on her hospital rounds, his smile would light up the room. Just being able to muster a smile was anything but routine for this seventy-six-year-old man. You see, the cancer had spread throughout his body. His death was imminent, and he knew it. It took every ounce of energy in his fragile body to open his eyes, thank her for coming in to see him, and remind her that she was his angel on earth.

The day before his body succumbed to the disease, he made a request, knowing it would probably be his last.

"My dear angel Dr. Becky," he said, "I have a last favor to ask of you."

"Of course," she said softly. "What can I do for you?"

"May I please see your feet and red toenails up close?"

Without hesitation Dr. Becky removed a high heel, hiked up her skirt to just above her knee, and positioned her perfectly manicured toes just a few inches from his face. His smile was priceless—she knew she'd never forget it.

The next day he left this world behind, along with the excruciating pain of his last few months. Following his death, his widow told Dr. Becky she was certain her husband had held on a few extra days, just to see his angel on earth a few more times. Then she and Becky embraced each other and cried together.

This was not the first time Dr. Becky cried with one of her patients or their families, and it certainly would not be the last. I've always been told that doctors must emotionally distance themselves from their patients. Personally, I've never understood how they could do that, and I guess neither has Becky. It's rare that we go out for dinner in Tucson without someone zeroing in and giving her a hug, then thanking her for changing or saving their life, or the life of one of their family members. I've been told by many of her patients that she's one of the few remaining doctors who take time to really listen and try to understand their problems, or even seem to care what they're going through.

Becky laughs with her patients and she cries with her patients. She invites them into our home and has been known to visit them at theirs. She's indeed a rare breed in the deteriorating world of medicine and managed care. Medicine has never been about the money to her – I'm certain of that. She has dedicated her life to serving others, and nothing will ever get in the way of that dedication.

You may be wondering why I chose to introduce this book with such personal stories. Quite simply, to me these stories convey the infinitely deep passion my wife carries for all things in life – including the writing of this book. This is her gift to others, a constellation of topics, ideas, and knowledge all rolled into a simple, easy to read adventure into the inner workings of the human body, mind, and spirit. It's educational and it's humorous. It will compel you to take a long, hard look at where you are in life and to make decisions about where you want to go. It will instill in you a sense of obligation to embrace and share its gift of knowledge with everyone you come in contact with. It will help you to believe that you can and should strive to make a difference in others' lives on many levels.

I've been distinctly blessed with the opportunity to watch and learn from Becky on a daily basis – from both a personal and professional perspective. I always marvel at the way she makes daily decisions based on how the end result will affect others, never lamenting about how those decisions might affect her. Her life philosophy has always been based on the principle that "If you do right by others, everything good will ultimately come back to you." This wonderful book is an extension of that principle and is her unique gift to the friends, family, and business associates she so deeply cherishes.

I'm confident you'll enjoy reading it as much as I did.

Introduction

At the age of three my son Kathan began exhibiting the upsetting symptoms of asthma. Pulmonary and allergy evaluations confirmed our worst fears. We were informed that during certain times of the year he would require a bronchial inhaler, nasal steroids, oral steroids, antibiotics, decongestants, and various allergy medications to combat his symptoms. Over time his breathing at night became so compromised that I had to keep a baby monitor in his room so I could track his breathing patterns as he slept.

When he was five years old he was playing in his room with his stepbrother Devin while the monitor was on. My husband Dan and I overheard Devin ask him, "What does your mom do for a job?"

Kathan snickered and said, "She looks at butts all day."

Devin said between giggles, "She does what?"

"She's a butt doctor! She looks at people's BUTTS all day long!"

To which Devin replied, "That is so-o-o weird!"

Dan and I didn't even try to contain our laughter. Since the word "gastroenterology" was too difficult to pronounce, from that point on my family lovingly referred to me as the "Butts and Guts" doctor.

When I informed my friend Jeano about my new nickname, he said, "As far as I'm concerned, you're just an Ass and Gas doctor." This is the same friend who showed up for his colonoscopy with his girlfriend's bright red lip imprints on his right butt cheek and an appropriately pointed red arrow on his left butt cheek indicating "insert here." Oh, the life of a GI doctor. Some of my neighbors call me the In and Out doctor and some call me GI Jane.

I've become accustomed to the humorous names, the jokes, and all the hilarious off-color comics people send me. I've included many of them in this book. Laughter in my profession can be the best medicine. And although my job and my nickname are a bit unusual for a woman, I do have a friend-- an attractive blond urologist—who's known as the Pecker Checker.

Like my friend the urologist, I love what I do. And like my friend Lenny Evans always says, I believe that "We were put on this earth to serve." I believe this statement to be universally true, and through my profession I've committed myself to serving others as my life's passion. I'm so grateful for my God-given talents. I care about my patients, many of whom have become my friends. Over the years, however, I've witnessed distressing events in the world of health care. Health care has evolved into "sick" care -- we're experiencing a true health crisis in America.

Today most people working in the health care industry focus on treating the symptoms of disease rather than preventing it. The reason is because it's significantly more profitable for medical companies to research and develop products that create customers for life than to develop products that solve underlying health issues.

In the past, a significant part of the health care industry focused on wellness and preventive care. This is no longer the case—with the consequence that people are becoming sicker and sicker. At times I feel paralyzed in my ability to offer truly adequate medical care. Unfortunately, for many Americans this crisis is connected with financial crisis. Last year in this country there were more bankruptcies filed than at any time in American history. Statistics indicate that a significant percentage of these bankruptcies were the result of family medical catastrophes. And prescription drugs represent the single largest monthly expense for the majority of Americans over the age of 65, averaging approximately $300 per month. All too often I see people forced to choose between buying food or filling their prescriptions.

Many people are aware of these hard truths and are getting sick and tired of being sick and tired. Many of us want to make a change but are stuck in our old habits and fear change. All too often, the fear of change or the fear of failure is stronger than the desire to make a change. This book can be a tool to help reignite that desire, alleviate that fear, and provide knowledge and direction to finally make a change. It's designed to help eliminate a lot of the excuses, the "if's" "and's" or "buts" when it comes to taking control of your health. I firmly believe that in most instances, optimal health and the necessary financial means to manage your own health can become realities if you simply make a decision to have them.

This book provides a first-hand look at my world and what I've experienced and ultimately discovered. It's intended to be an educational tool -- a why and how-to guide, if you will -- to help you achieve and share the gift of optimal wellness.

Chapter 1

THE SICKNESS REVOLUTION

The sickness revolution has spurred a continual confrontation between the frustrated patient and the frustrated doctor. Diagnostic dilemmas are rampant and sometimes the doctor just doesn't have a clue what's wrong with the patient. Doctors are frustrated that they can't adequately help their patients and furthermore, their once lucrative careers have fallen prey to the financially controlling insurance companies, managed care industry, Health Maintenance Organizations (HMO's) and the continual rising costs of the medical malpractice organizations. Most physicians embrace medicine for the right reasons, and no matter what obstacles they encounter they remain in their profession because they truly want to help people. Like any profession however, less than honorable individuals can give the whole profession a tarnished appearance and throughout history, there has been an evolving perception regarding doctors and their true abilities and intentions. One of my patients considered herself an **expert** on what doctors were really all about. She had **eight** subspecialty physicians that cared for her and when I asked her what she did for a living she said, "I am a career patient". Having multiple doctors at any given-time had been part of her life since she was twelve. She gave me the following joke and I have to tell you it made me laugh--a lot!

What the Doctor says

What the Doctor really means

"This medication should fix you up."

"The drug salesman guaranteed that it kills all symptoms."

"Let's see how it develops."

"Maybe in a few days it will grow into something that can be cured."

"This should be taken care of right away."

"I've planned a trip to Hawaii next month and this is so easy and profitable that I want to schedule multiple high paying tests before it cures itself."

"Wellllll, what have we here..."

Since he hasn't the foggiest notion of what it is, the Doctor is hoping you will give him a clue.

"We'll see."

"First I have to check my malpractice insurance."

"Let me check your medical history."
"I want to see if you've paid your last bill before spending any more time with you."

"Why don't we make another appointment later in the week."
"I need the money, so I'm charging you for another office visit."

"I really can't recommend seeing a chiropractor."
"I hate those guys mooching in on our fees."

"Hmmmmmmmmmmmmmmmmmmmmmmmm."
Since he hasn't the faintest idea of what to do, he is trying to appear thoughtful while hoping the nurse will interrupt. (Proctologist also say this alot.)

"We have some good news and some bad news."
The good news is he's going to buy that new BMW, and the bad news is you're going to pay for it.

"Let me schedule you for some tests."
"I have a 40% interest in the lab."

"I'd like to have my associate look at you."
"He's going through a messy divorce and owes me a small fortune."

"How are we today?"
"I feel great. You, on the other hand, look like hell."

"If it doesn't clear up in a week, give me a call."
"I don't know what the hell it is. Maybe it will go away by itself."

"Well, we're not feeling so well today, are we?"
"I can't remember your name, nor why you are here."

"I'd like to run some more tests."
"I can't figure out what's wrong. Maybe the kid in the lab can solve this one."

"Do you suppose all of this stress could be affecting your nerves?"
He thinks you are crazy and is hoping to find a psychiatrist who will split fees.

"If those symptoms persist, call for an appointment."

"I've never heard of anything so disgusting. Thank God I'm off next week."

"There is a lot of that going around."
"My God, that's the third one this week. I'd better learn something about this."

In my twelve years as a gastrointestinal specialist, the variety of illness and disease I've seen is absolutely staggering. Each year I witness a continual decline in my patients' overall state of health. My clinics are constantly overbooked with people suffering from chronic intestinal and liver problems, and in many cases traditional medical solutions provide only temporary relief. For me, prescribing more and more drugs is like slapping a band-aid over a serious wound.

We've become a nation of pill poppers. We have pills to help us sleep, pills to keep us awake, pills to combat depression, pills to ease anxiety, pills to make us go to the bathroom, and pills to "stop us up." With approximately three billion prescriptions being written yearly in this country, I find myself asking "when is enough, enough"? What I've seen is that prescription drugs all too often simply mask the symptoms of illness and disease, and all too seldom support the strengthening and healing process so essential for the body to achieve clinical remission and optimal health. Drugs rarely if ever address the fact that most of us are nutritionally depleted and many of us are nutritionally bankrupt. Drugs don't address the issue of toxicity in the body. In fact, I believe that often they add to or even create more of a problem.

Pharmaceuticals can play a temporary therapeutic role, but *I believe that if you nutritionally replenish the body and help the body internally cleanse itself at a cellular level, it's possible to achieve optimal health and wellness beyond your wildest dreams.* I know in my heart that this is true. This type of healing is not a band-aid approach to health but a lifestyle approach that puts each of us individually in control. I've witnessed this personally, and in countless friends, family members and patients. Everyone needs to know this option exists, but very few people understand it or want to discuss it. That's why I am dedicated to educating anyone willing to listen and learn about this very simple yet crucial concept.

Cleansing the body at an internal level is a hot topic, and for good reason. It makes perfect sense. Ours is a highly toxic world, and unless you live in a bubble, your body is continually suffering the detrimental effects of dangerous, often deadly poisons. Our environment is full of herbicides, petrochemicals, hydrocarbons, heavy metals, food additives, and synthetic drugs and these overabundant toxins can have an adverse effect on your cells, internal organs, and ultimately, your state of health.

Animals raised for consumption in factory farms are often injected with hormones, steroids, and antibiotics. Over 20 million pounds of antibiotics were injected into our farm animals last year alone. There are so many insecticides and pesticides on our fruits and vegetables that these noxious chemicals have become part of our food chain. Adults and sadly even our children are chronically exposed to these substances. Everything we eat or drink has a direct effect on our health -- it all starts within the liver and intestinal tract. The typical American diet is destroying our digestive systems and leading to other chronic problems in the body. I believe we are literally eating ourselves to death and we don't even know it.

America is in a true health crisis, and there's no end in sight. Cardiovascular disease is epidemic, 44 million people suffer from arthritis, 18 million have diabetes, 17 million suffer from asthma, 1 in 8 women develop breast cancer, and 18 million children are obese. Diseases, many of them preventable, are out of control, and for the first time in generations we're experiencing a decline in life span because of our deteriorating lifestyles. Health care has become sick care, and the medical insurance and pharmaceutical industries are the primary beneficiaries of this horrific trend.

Sickness has become an accepted way of life for millions of Americans, and we've actually convinced ourselves that this is supposed to happen as we age. Our bodies are falling apart and our nutritional status is suffering. America is one of the most over-fed yet undernourished societies in the world, and even though we're one of the most technologically advanced societies on earth, we're the sickest! David Letterman said it with a smile when announcing his "top ten" list, focusing on the outlandish food portions that Americans ingest.

DAVID LETTERMAN'S TOP TEN QUESTIONS
TO ASK YOURSELF BEFORE EATING
A 15-POUND CHEESEBURGER

10. **"Does this restaurant have a defibrillator?"**
9. **"Am I that hungry or should I just order the 12-pound cheeseburger?"**
8. **"Does it come with fries?"**
7. **"Would it be easier to eat 60 quarter pounders?"**
6. **"Can I get it on a low carb bun?"**
5. **"How expensive is it to be buried in a piano case?"**
4. **"What am I going to have for dessert?"**
3. **"Why is everybody looking at me?"**
2. **"What would Jesus do?"**

1. "Can I super-size that?!!!!"

I have several patients who moved to the United States from Europe and other countries only to have their excellent health deteriorate rapidly. This decline is coincident with their exposure to the American lifestyle, which includes processed, injected, chemically altered food and many other components of our abundantly toxic environment. They are clueless as why they're suddenly gaining excessive weight and experiencing severe digestive problems.

Chapter 2

CLEANSING IS NOT JUST FOR THE COLON ANY MORE

I've performed thousands of colonoscopies in the last decade and evaluated at least 14,000 butts! We're all creatures of habit, so please be careful not to drop your keys if you happen to be walking in front of me. And if you're a former patient who sees me on the street and says hello, please don't take offense if I don't remember your face.

In order to perform a colonoscopy, which is a look at the large intestine with a small-diameter camera inside a flexible tube, a patient must go through a colon preparation the day before. You'll either drink a special electrolyte solution or swallow a bunch of pills that "clean you out" from top to bottom.

Once you initiate this type of cleansing, I recommend not making any plans and positioning yourself a few seconds from the closest bathroom. One consistent pattern I've discovered over the years is that patients who successfully eliminate all of the toxic waste from their colons at the least feel better and in some cases feel wonderful for several days after the procedure. This all makes perfect sense to me, because despite our body's natural ability to detoxify itself, excess toxins often remain and fester in the large intestine.

The question I always asked myself was this: "Beyond just cleaning out the colon, what if there was a way to help the body cleanse on an internal level, thus helping all of our vital organs and cells?" I was not aware of any approach to bringing about this end, but I knew that if I could discover something effective, the results could be life-changing. For years I've have been on a quest to find a natural approach to accomplishing this.

Cleansing or detoxifying is our body's natural process for eliminating harmful toxins. Our body will eliminate toxins through the liver (its primary detoxifying organ), colon, urinary tract, sweat glands, skin pores, and the lymphatic system. The liver is the gateway to internal health, and when the liver is overworked, this has a dramatic effect on how we feel. As we're exposed to more and more toxins, our body's natural ability to detoxify becomes strained and our internal body suffers. This often leads to infections, fatigue, constipation, irritable bowel, gas, bloating, aches and pains, headaches, altered sleep patterns, and an endless array of other unpleasant symptoms. With all of the digestive problems I encounter in my practice, there's no question in my mind that dehydration and the ingestion of nutrient-poor, chemically processed toxic foods is at the root of many of Americans' gastrointestinal problems.

Because our soil is poisoned with chemicals and pollutants and is continually stripped of its nutrient base, many of the foods grown from it aren't supplying our bodies with the necessary nutrients--primarily minerals--for our bodies to perform optimally. Minerals are absolutely essential for 90% of our bodily functions. *You cannot effectively absorb vitamins and other essential nutrients if your body lacks the necessary mineral base to support them.* The nutritionally bankrupt body is an invitation to illness and disease and invites a wide range of intestinal and hepatic (liver) disorders.

Issues related to the bowels often go unreported and more often than not are never even discussed. It's accepted cocktail conversation to talk about cardiac- related chest pain or even open heart surgery--"everyone is having it"--but it's not appropriate to mention how much gas you had after eating a plate of greasy tacos and a smothered bean burrito for lunch. Social conversation usually does not include the topics of diarrhea, constipation, hemorrhoids, or flatulence.

The major exception is when people get around a GI doctor. On social occasions, its' astonishing how often my husband and I find ourselves in grossly detailed conversation about someone's intestinal problems. Some people don't even wait for dessert to be served -- they just lay it on you during the main course. I've become accustomed to this type of verbal catharsis. Because I know how much someone's life can be altered if his or her intestinal tract is out of whack, I never reject an invitation to engage in discussion regarding my world of Butts & Guts. My husband has learned to listen graciously to these conversations and will often encourage them in order to incite the humor, sick jokes and grotesque stories that often follow.

Many people have quietly become obsessed with their intestinal function because their bowels are in such disarray. These problems often run and can even ruin your life, and I hear about them every day. Many individuals plan their day according to which bathrooms they are familiar with. I hear things in my office like "The Safeway bathrooms are much nicer than Trader Joe's", or "I only shop at Basha's because their bathrooms are clean and easy to get to in a hurry." Some people don't leave the house on days they know their bowels are acting up -- appointments and social events are determined by how their intestines are performing. I receive dozens of e-mails and phone calls weekly about life-altering bowel problems. Virtually none of us has been spared suffering from some type of digestive distress.

Chapter 3

DIGESTION SUGGESTIONS

When I started my medical practice in Tucson, a nurse at one of the local hospitals gave me this joke, one of my favorites:

Two doctors opened an office in Tucson, Arizona, and put up a sign that read: Dr. Smith and Dr. Becky Natrajan, Psychiatry and Proctology. The conservative Tucson town council was not too happy with that sign, so the doctors changed it to Hysterias and Posteriors. The town council frowned again so they tried Schizoids and Hemorrhoids. No go. Next they tried Catatonics and High Colonics. Thumbs down again. Then came Manic-Depressives and Anal-Retentives. Still not good. How about Minds and Behinds? Unacceptable. Lost Souls and Assholes? Absolutely no go. Neither were Analysis and Anal Cysts, Nuts and Butts, Freaks and Cheeks, or Loons and Moons.

By now at their wits' end, the doctors gave the Tucson council one last option: Dr. Smith and Dr. Becky Natrajan: Odds and Ends. Approved.

The digestive tract is the key to our internal state of health, because literally everything we put into our mouths has an effect on our cells and vital organs. When our digestive system isn't functioning well, our entire internal body and overall state of health suffers. Why this happens is like the Chicken and the Egg riddle when it comes to what came first. It seems to be a perpetuating vicious cycle.

The root of the problem is that our digestive systems face new challenges daily. Nutritionally bankrupt fast foods, highly processed foods, and foods riddled with chemicals can overburden the liver and force the digestive tract to work overtime in order to extract nutrients. Poor digestion may well be the number-one factor contributing to toxicity accumulation in the body, and can lead to a disruption in the body's bacterial balance. This disruption can allow intestinal overgrowth of harmful bacteria and yeast, which in turn can cause serious gas and bloating. Meals that were once enjoyable suddenly leave us feeling uncomfortable and fatigued. I often have patients tell me they're literally "afraid to eat." Imagine how traumatic it would be to live in fear of food.

Poor digestion is often associated with the following:
- Gas and Bloating
- Constipation, diarrhea, or a constant irregularity of the bowel
- Gallbladder dysfunction and disease
- Food allergies
- Obesity

- Fatigue and poor sleep cycles
- Headaches
- Liver disease
- Immune disorders
- Cancer
- Endocrine disorders

Ensuring a healthy digestive system is crucial to attaining optimal health on all levels. Without sufficient physical and enzymatic breakdown of foods, the essential nutrients our cells require to function properly won't be available. Digestive disturbances can be acute and painfully obvious. Some intestinal ills disappear quickly, but some can become chronic and have the potential to cause a health emergency.

According to the holistic science of Ayurveda, digestion is the cornerstone of health. Ayurveda, which originates from India, is more than five thousand years old. "Ayur" means life, and "Ved" means knowledge. This "life knowledge" utilizes the complete balance of the body, mind, and spirit, including the emotions, on all levels. According to this tradition, health is the balance of elements such as air, earth, fire, and water. Illness represents an imbalance of any particular element. Ayurveda treats illness at its source rather than at the level of symptoms, and helps an individual take responsibility for his or her health and well-being. Treating illness at its source allows the body to heal more naturally and effectively.

There are two aspects to food and nutrition in Ayurveda. One is the physical food you eat, digest, and assimilate. In this process, the vital organs of your digestive system play a big role. The second aspect is what you consume through your mind-body. This concept is a huge factor when it comes to the gut. What you see, hear, taste, smell, feel, and think are all incredibly important and impact your health considerably. The mind-gut connection is very powerful -- for example, stress plays a key role in digestive health.

When my patients are under stress, my waiting room is packed. Irritable Bowel Syndrome is flaring, gastric upset is frequent, and diffuse abdominal pain with bloating is out of control. I've also noticed that during stressful times of the year, mainly around the holidays, I see a lot more new and chronic Crohn's and ulcerative colitis patients. I receive dozens of reflux-related phone calls during tax time, and when college students are taking final exams, it seems half the campus suffers with diarrhea. However, by addressing brain chemistry and stress on a nutritional level, many positive health results can occur, especially within the digestive tract.

I consider Dr. John Gray one of the leading experts in the area of balanced brain chemistry. Dr. Gray is known for his Mars/Venus series of books and is a nationally known relationship therapist and motivational speaker. In his recent book *The Mars & Venus Diet & Exercise Solution,* he accurately describes how cleansing and nourishing your body and brain with the right balance of high-grade nutrients including amino acids, minerals, and vitamins will optimize the function of your liver and digestive system. A healthy digestive tract will absorb better, and a healthy liver will utilize nutrients more efficiently, allowing for the production of healthy brain chemicals that facilitate better brain chemistry.

Virtually everyone will experience digestive stress at some point in his or her life. If your mental state is not in balance I can guarantee that your gut will react negatively, and digestive disturbances may become your life partner. If you get your brain back in balance, you'll be able to make better health decisions and eliminate cravings that aggravate the gut.

The American diet has created a chronic disruption to our digestive systems, harming our children's intestinal function and general state of health. Pediatric GI doctors are overwhelmed with young patients, and many of these children require extensive medical evaluation. If a child is constantly eating processed, nutritionally bankrupt, chemically preserved and altered foods, what in the world do you think is going to happen with their digestive systems? What do you think is going to happen with their brain chemistry and their ability to focus?

In many instances when children are suffering from intestinal distress, they don't need the expensive, emotionally draining medical work-up, they need a consistent dosage of organic, high-grade absorbable protein, minerals, amino acids, and vitamins. If you give these growing bodies and brains the proper balance of pure and essential nutrients, it's almost miraculous what can happen. Our children and grandchildren need some balance in a world that's constantly marketing the next nutritionally depleted and addictive fast food item.

It's important to understand that our quality of life is determined by our daily choices and that we all have the power to improve our health. Health in many instances is a matter of choice. If you choose to be ill, then nothing in this modern world can help you. One of my biggest frustrations is dealing with patients who are addicted to their illness. They use it as a crutch, they use it to get disability. They use it to get out of jury duty and they use it to make other people guests at their "pity party." They use it to get attention from their spouse and family.

I've learned not to allow my blood pressure to hit stroke range while relentlessly and fruitlessly attempting to help these individuals. So please remember, if you choose to go out in this world and share the gift of health and wellness with others, you cannot help those who have an addiction to their illness and don't want to help themselves. Realizing this will allow you to avoid the headaches caused by banging your head against the wall.

Chapter 4

THE ANGRY
IRRITABLE BOWEL

One of my patients with irritable bowel syndrome handed me this story just before I sedated him for his colonoscopy. He told me he'd discovered quite some time ago that beans almost cost him his marriage, and he hadn't eaten a legume in over ten years!

Baked Beans

Once upon a time, there lived a man who had a fierce passion for baked beans, which unfortunately always had an embarrassing and somewhat lively effect on him. He met a girl and fell in love. When they became engaged, he figured his problem would put a strain on their marriage so he made the supreme sacrifice and gave up beans.

Shortly after that they were married. A few months later, on his birthday, his car broke down on the way home from work. Since they lived in the country, he called his wife and told her he'd be late because he had to walk home. On the way he passed a diner, and the wonderful aroma of baked beans overwhelmed him. Since he still had several miles to go, he figured he could walk off any ill effects before he got home. It was, after all, his birthday. So he went in and ordered, and before leaving had three extra-large helpings of baked beans.

All the way home he putt-putted. By the time he arrived he felt reasonably safe. His wife met him at the door and cried out, "Darling, I have the most wonderful surprise for you for dinner tonight!" She put a blindfold on him, led him to his chair at the head of the table, and made him promise not to peek. At this point he was beginning to feel another one coming on. Just as his wife was about to remove the blindfold, the telephone rang.

She made him promise not to peek until she returned, and away she went to answer the phone. While she was gone, he seized the opportunity, shifted his weight to one leg, and let go. It was not only loud but also ripe as a rotten egg. He had difficulty breathing, so he felt for his napkin and fanned the air about him. He had just started to feel better when another urge struck him. He raised his leg and RRIIPPP !!! It sounded like a diesel engine revving and smelled worse. To keep from gagging, he tried fanning his arms, hoping the smell would dissipate. He got another urge. This was a real blue- ribbon winner -- the windows shook, the dishes on the table rattled, and a minute later the flowers on the table wilted.

CHAPTER 4

Still blindfolded, he heard the phone farewells, neatly laid his napkin on his lap, and folded his hands on top of it. Smiling contentedly, he was the picture of innocence when his wife walked in. She apologized for taking so long and asked if he had peeked at the dinner table. When he assured her he hadn't, she removed the blindfold and yelled, "SURPRISE!!!"

To his horror, there were twelve pale-faced shocked dinner guests seated around the table for his surprise birthday party.

-- Anonymous

I receive thousands of calls and e-mails regarding the irritable bowel. Irritable bowel syndrome (IBS), also referred to as "spastic bowel," is one of the most common ailments I see in my practice. IBS is associated with gas, bloating, and significant abdominal pain accompanied by either diarrhea or constipation. In my opinion, 99% of the population deals with IBS at some point in their lives. With many people, no matter what they eat, it causes severe gas and bloating. Patient sometimes bring in a picture of their magical growing abdomen. "Doctor, my belly is flat in the morning and then I blow up like a balloon by three p.m." "I feel and look like I'm six months' pregnant!" And the pictures I see are truly astonishing. I've seen flat tummies that grew to basketball-size in just a few hours.

The irritable bowel is filled with noxious gas. The movement and contraction of the intestine becomes irregular, thus making you and your digestive tract irritable. IBS is often painful, its etiology an underlying motility disorder. To understand this, you need to understand what intestinal motility is.

Motility is movement, and intestinal movement is called peristalsis. You need normal peristalsis of all parts of the intestinal tract to attain and maintain normal digestion and elimination. The esophagus needs peristalsis to propel food from the mouth to the stomach. The stomach needs peristalsis to aid in the breakdown of food so it can be propelled into the small intestine. The small bowel is anywhere from 18 to 24 feet long, and peristalsis allows for the absorption of nutrients and the passage of waste products into the colon. The colon needs peristalsis to allow for water regulation and the expulsion of waste.

There's a tremendous sequence of motility events involved with digestion. When this sequence is altered, you have abnormal elimination, foul-smelling gas, bloating, and quite often, significant abdominal pain. Your bowel is irritable, you're irritable, and usually everyone around you is irritable. The problem can be life-controlling. Many of my patients live their lives according to the current state of their irritable bowel.

FLATULENCE

In the female: An embarrassing by-product of digestion. In the male: An endless source of entertainment, self-expression, and male bonding.

Flatus, flatulence, gas, farts -- whatever you call it, we all do it. Some of us vehemently deny it, some of us do it regularly, and some of us can't leave the house! In my world of butts and guts, flatulence is a welcome post-colonoscopy sound and recovery room nurses happily encourage this act so patients can expel any excess air that accumulated during the procedure. Men especially welcome this invitation, since farting in public seems to be an acceptable rite of passage for so many of them.

A belch is but a gust of wind that cometh from the heart. But should it take a downward trend, turneth into a fart.

-- Anonymous

Too much gas at inappropriate times could signal tremendous imbalance in your digestive tract. There may be bacterial or yeast overgrowth. Some parasitic infections such as giardia can cause excessive amounts of foul-smelling gas. Excess carbohydrates can contribute to severe gas, which could jeopardize even the most solid of relationships. I have couples that sleep in separate rooms, and more than once an argument has erupted in my office over the issue of excessive flatulence.

My all-time bizarre flatulence experience occurred when a patient brought me an audiotape of her gas sounds! She told me that something was seriously wrong with her, and if I listened to her farts I could figure it out. I assured her that there was indeed something seriously wrong with her, but the answer would not be found in her audio file. This poem is in loving tribute to her.

A fart can be quiet,
A fart can be loud,
Some leave a powerful
poisonous cloud.

A fart can be short,
Or a fart can be long,
Some farts have been known
To sound just like a song.

Some farts do not smell,
While others are vile,
A fart may pass quickly
Or linger awhile.

A fart can create
A most curious medley,

A fart can be harmless,
Or silent but deadly.

A fart can occur
In a number of places,
And leave just about everyone
With strange looks on their faces.

From wide-open prairies
To small elevators,
A fart will find all of us
Sooner or later.

So be not afraid
Of the invisible gas,
For always remember
That farts, too, shall pass
                    -- Anonymous

In order to uncover my patients' issues related to gas, bloating, and irritable bowel, I immediately hone in on what their eating habits are. Sometimes we uncover the obvious, as a daily pot of coffee, a six-pack of soda, or a dozen raw jalapenos does not promote a happy digestive tract. I often point out to my patients that if you eat rapidly, irregularly, or don't provide nourishment to the digestive tract on a regular schedule, the bowels will behave in the same manner you treat them. Irregular patterns create an irregular bowel, and if you skip meals, avoid water, or eat nutritionally deficient foods low in fiber, your bowels will thank you with an uproar of unhealthy and often embarrassing symptoms.

Many of my patients tell me they eat "very healthfully" and they just can't understand why their intestines are so out of control. My question to them is, "What, exactly, do you mean by 'healthfully?'" If you eat *only* organic foods, you're ahead of the game and I commend you. In our family we try to eat organic whenever possible, but like so many Americans we're constantly on the go and forced to eat food that's a far cry from pure.

Our overly processed and preserved foods are definitely *not* pure or straight from nature. When was the last time you saw a chicken nugget, bagel bite, Big Mac, Lunchable, or pizza roll in nature? Observe what our kids are eating for their all-important brain- stimulating first meal of the day: frozen waffles, frozen pancakes, sugar- laden cereals, donuts, pastries, pop-tarts, and other cardboard-like substances. Starting out your day with lifeless foods promotes an unhappy gut and unhealthy brain chemistry. Without a balanced dietary program with essential nutrients for the growing brain, the initials ADD and ADHD may become awfully familiar labels. Nutritionally bankrupt foods are also responsible for the growing incidence of irritable bowel syndrome in kids, not to mention all of the other digestive ailments that are plaguing our innocent pediatric population.

We're all intestinally challenged. Think about it: if you had a nice "healthy" salad for lunch, was the lettuce sprayed with pesticides or insecticides? Keep in mind that in this country our fruits and veggies are often laden with pesticides, herbicides, and insecticides. Last time I checked, many of these were no safer than some illegal poisons. Often these fruits and veggies are sprayed several times, right up until you pick them out of the produce section of your local grocery store.

Remember the quaint sound of thunder and rain just prior to the automated spraying of the grocery store fruit and vegetable display. Did you really think that was just water? What about that baked chicken or filet mignon you had yesterday? Was it with or without hormones, antibiotics, or steroids? The factory farm industry has been injecting our animals with these chemicals for years. What about that seafood you had for dinner? Was it with or without mercury, and was the fish wild or farm-raised? What about that water you're drinking? Is the bottled water your family uses regulated for its safety and purity? Some community water facilities are suffering the effects of people flushing their old pharmaceuticals down the toilet -- thus allowing the breakdown products of these drugs to circulate back into the water supply. Your water may contain the breakdown products of antidepressants and steroids. Obviously, all of the above can adversely affect the digestive tract and consequently the health of the entire body. The bottom line is that the digestive tract craves balance, but poor diets, nutritionally bankrupt foods, abundant toxins, dehydration, and stress will cause severe imbalance. And where there's imbalance, there's bloating, gas, pain, diarrhea, and constipation.

IBS is a constellation of symptoms and is very often a diagnosis of exclusion, meaning that you may need a few tests to rule out other intestinal issues before you're diagnosed with an irritable bowel. In my many years of practice I've prescribed every medication appropriate for IBS, and the results are usually temporary and ultimately disappointing. Getting to the root of the problem is essential. When you get back to basics, help the body cleanse, and put high-grade absorbable nutrients including fiber and purified water into the digestive system, wonderful things will start happening. Get into a healthy lifestyle that assists the bowels in effective digestion, absorption, and elimination.

The following recommendations are remarkably helpful in addressing the irritable bowel:
- Drink several glasses of purified water daily.
- Avoid all sodas and caffeinated products.
- Avoid tobacco products and excess alcohol.
- Eat raw organic vegetables and fruits. In severe cases of gas and bloating increase the raw veggies and decrease the fruit intake. Raw organic foods contain living enzymes and phytonutrients that help the bacterial balance of your intestinal tract.

- Eat slowly and regularly. Chew your foods well. (If you eat erratically and rapidly your bowels will behave the same way. Racing through a drive-through and eating in your car is an invitation to extreme gas and bloating. Don't teach your children this habit.)

- Include more fiber in your diet and add in grains, flax seed, or psyllium seed. Introduce supplemental fiber slowly to decrease any initial excess gas.

- Other foods supportive of intestinal balance include raw garlic, radishes, fresh ginger root, and cruciferous veggies such as broccoli, brussel sprouts, cauliflower, and cabbage. Steaming and softening the cruciferous veggies will decrease the gas associated with introduction of these items.

- Eat less refined sugars and carbohydrates. Excess carbohydrates can fuel microorganisms such as yeast.

- If larger meals make you feel uncomfortable, eat smaller, more frequent meals.

- Some irritable bowels respond well to the elimination of milk from the diet.

- Avoid products sweetened with aspartame, sorbitol, or xylitol (diet drinks and many chewing gums).

- Avoid MSG, an unnecessary source of sodium that can cause intestinal upset and headaches.

- Ingest probiotics such as lactobacillus and acidophilus.

- Use fennel seed and/or peppermint oil for gas and spasm-related discomfort.

- Keep a food log to research possible food intolerances. List daily foods and the digestive symptoms that occurred afterwards. This may be helpful in determining which items should be eliminated from the diet.
- When shopping for poultry or meats, buy products that are free from antibiotic, hormone, or steroid injections.
- Avoid farm-raised seafood and try to purchase seafood that is caught in the wild.
- Avoid fast foods with high fat content.
- Embrace a program to help with stress reduction such as meditation, biofeedback, or yoga.

Chapter 5

LOVE YOUR LIVER

The liver is one of the most important detoxifying organs in our miraculous bodies. Our large intestine is a conduit for elimination of waste, but the liver is responsible for the breakdown of toxic substances and is the cleanser and filter for the bloodstream. The liver is quite sophisticated and secretes vital digestive juices that help us process and properly absorb essential nutrients. In today's world, our livers are forced to work harder than ever. When the liver is overtaxed, it will greatly impact how you look and feel and have a direct and immediate effect on your overall state of health.

A woman walked up to a little old man rocking in a chair on his porch.

"I couldn't help noticing how content you look," *she said. "What's your secret for a long, happy life?"*

"I smoke three packs of cigarettes a day," he *said. "I drink a case of whiskey a week, eat fatty* *over-processed nutritionally deficient foods, and* *never exercise."*

"That's amazing," the woman said. "How old are *you?'*

"Thirty-two," he said.

Chronic liver disease and cirrhosis (scarring of the liver) rank fourth among the leading disease-related causes of death for Americans between the ages of 25 and 44. Since everything we ingest, breathe, and absorb through our skin must be refined and detoxified by the liver, special attention to cleansing, nutrition, and hydration is necessary to keep the liver revitalized.

The liver performs many unique and important metabolic tasks as it processes carbohydrates, proteins, fats, and minerals to be used in maintaining normal bodily functions. Almost all of the blood that leaves the stomach and intestines must pass through the liver before reaching the rest of the body. The liver is strategically placed to process nutrients and drugs absorbed from the digestive tract into forms that are easier for the rest of the body to use.

The liver plays a principal role in removing toxins from the blood, whether they are ingested or internally produced. It attempts to convert all of these substances into a form that can be easily eliminated from the body. The liver can chemically modify pharmaceuticals, rendering them more or less active. The liver also makes bile, a greenish yellow fluid that contains detergent-like substances essential for the digestion of fats. The liver produces many proteins involved with blood clotting and immune-system function. It produces certain hormones, manufactures cholesterol, and helps balance the endocrine system.

The liver is a highly sophisticated organ, and liver dysfunction manifests in several ways. Abnormal liver function can lead to the abnormal metabolism of fats, resulting in the elevation of triglyceride and bad cholesterol (LDL) levels and the lowering of good cholesterol (HDL) levels. Steatohepatitis (fatty deposits within the liver) is quite common and can lead to irreversible liver damage. Liver dysfunction can also lead to various digestive problems, unstable blood sugar levels, immune dysfunction, nervous system dysfunction, and hormonal imbalance.

One of the essential things I learned during my medical training was that the liver is a remarkably resilient, regenerative organ that is easily improved. However, when the liver is chemically overloaded it can deteriorate, and its ability to filter becomes compromised or stagnated.

A 45 year-old woman came to my office when she noticed her eyes were yellow and her urine had turned very dark. Her liver tests were markedly elevated, and upon examination she was extremely jaundiced (yellowing of the skin secondary to liver disease). Because of numerous medical problems, she was taking 16 different prescription drugs and an adverse drug reaction developed that nearly killed her. The offending drugs were eliminated, and once she started nutritionally replenishing her body, her health turned around completely. Her

liver began functioning properly, and her skin and urine color returned to normal. Her liver required the additional nutritional support to aid in the process of strengthening its own detoxifying capabilities.

A strong liver means improved digestion. A strong liver means better metabolism and fat-burning ability. If the body is flooded with all of the trace minerals, amino acids, and vitamins that it needs, the now healthier liver can better utilize these nutrients -- thus improving health on all levels. A balanced nutritional program with adequate calories, proteins, fats, and carbohydrates can actually help the damaged liver to regenerate new liver cells. In fact, with many liver diseases, nutrition becomes an essential, accepted form of treatment.

If you help your liver revitalize, fatigue will become a thing of the past. Healthy brain chemistry becomes part of your future. A healthy liver promotes healthy thyroid function, and when the thyroid comes alive your metabolism and energy levels escalate. If you help the liver, a cascade of positive events will take place on an internal level. Your body can effectively digest fats and protein and convert these nutrients into healthy brain chemicals. When your brain chemistry is aligned, you'll make healthier food selections – you'll tend to not overeat or crave nutritionally bankrupt junk food. Your brain will naturally guide your choices, and increased energy will manifest into increased cardiovascular support and the urge to exercise. An increase in metabolism will help with your body's natural ability to burn fat and develop lean muscle.

The liver has two detoxification pathways, phase one and phase two. The work of each of these phases requires specific vitamins and minerals. These vitamins and minerals in turn need other nutrients -- phytochemicals and amino acids -- to help them do their job.

During phase one this pathway converts a toxic chemical to one that is less harmful, but free radicals are formed. Free radicals are unstable particles that react with the body and damage cells. If too many free radicals are made, they can harm the liver cells. In order to eliminate or reduce these free radicals, our bodies need support from food containing high-quality antioxidants and phytochemicals. The antioxidants beta-carotene, vitamins C and E, selenium, and many different phytochemicals are found in fruits, vegetables, and whole grains. One of the most important antioxidants is the amino acid glutathione, which is produced by the healthy liver. The B vitamins including thiamine (Vitamin B1), riboflavin (Vitamin B2), nicotinamide (Vitamin B3), calcium pantothenate (Vitamin B5), pyridoxine (Vitamin B6), cyanocobalamin (Vitamin B12), folic acid, biotin, and inositol are also very important in this phase one process.

During phase two the liver adds a substance to the now less harmful toxin, making it water-soluble so it can then be moved out of the body via the urine or feces. During this process the liver requires sulphur containing amino acids and nutrients such as glycine, glutamine, choline, and inositol. The cruciferous vegetables, raw garlic, and leeks are all excellent sources of natural sulphur and enhance phase two detoxification.

Many cultures use liver tonics to support healthy liver function. These tonics are often a mixture of the natural ingredients listed above that support both phases of liver detoxification. Milk thistle and green tea have also been used in many cultures to support the functional integrity of the liver. When the liver is supported, fat metabolism is more efficient, but if the liver is overburdened and dysfunctional, fatty accumulation can occur within the organ itself. NASH, or nonalcoholic steatohepatitis (fatty liver) is becoming more common as the trend of obesity overtakes our society. Many people who carry excess visceral fat (protuberant fatty accumulation in the abdominal area) also have a fatty liver. If left unattended, fatty liver can lead to inflammation and scarring of the liver. It can be quite difficult to lose weight if the liver is fatty and not functioning optimally. By naturally supporting liver detoxification, the liver will restore its fat-flushing abilities, aiding the body in overall weight control.

Supporting these two phases of detoxification gives our body a fighting chance against all of the chemicals and toxins that continually bombard us. Support your liver and live longer!

Chapter 6
REFLUX, REGURGITATION, AND FRUSTRATION

A big fat greasy cheeseburger was waiting in the stomach to be digested when suddenly a shot of whiskey came down. The burger figured: Okay, I'll let him pass, there's no hurry.

Two minutes later another shot of whiskey came by and the burger let him pass too, but two minutes later when the next one got there, the burger stopped him.

"What's going on out there?" he asked.

"Why, there's a big party up there!" the whiskey said. "It's great! They are having the best time!!!"

and the burger said, "Great, I'll run up and check it out!"

The digestive tract is an elegant, delicate, and sensitive system. If you put garbage in, you'll get garbage back and upper intestinal problems can surface quickly. If you have stomach or esophagus problems you may be in need of an upper endoscopy. This is a procedure performed by a qualified gastroenterologist in order to directly visualize the upper intestinal tract. Fortunately, you're comfortably sedated for the procedure. Your GI doctor will take a small flexible tube that has a fiber optic video camera inside and gently glide it over the tongue and into the esophagus to visualize the lining of the esophagus, stomach, and upper small bowel. The images are projected onto a large TV screen. There are many reasons why you may require an upper endoscopy, one of the most common being significant reflux.

Millions of Americans suffer from GERD -- gastro-esophageal reflux disease. Most of us know this problem as chronic heartburn, indigestion, or regurgitation. Heartburn can be very uncomfortable and can lead to chronic esophageal problems. GERD can exacerbate underlying lung problems and cause adult-onset asthma. Reflux is also linked to chronic cough, laryngitis, hoarseness, loss of dental enamel, and bad breath.

When you swallow, the lower esophageal sphincter — a circular band of muscle around the bottom part of your esophagus — relaxes to let food and liquid flow into your stomach. When it relaxes at any other time, stomach acids and enzymes rise back up into your esophagus, even if you're in an upright position. Reflux is usually worse when you're bent over or lying down. Some factors that can cause the lower esophageal sphincter to relax abnormally include:

- Fatty foods
- Chocolate, caffeine, onions, spicy foods
- Some medications
- Alcohol

- Large meals
- Lying down soon after eating
- Smoking

Heartburn can be exacerbated by a hiatal hernia (herniation of the stomach above the diaphragm). Reflux can cause a burning sensation in the chest and induce spasms that can result in significant, sometimes intolerable chest pain. Chest pain should always be taken seriously. If your heart checks out okay, then reflux-induced spasms may be the cause of the pain. If these gastric juices continue to wash up into the esophagus, the lining of the esophagus can break down and will sometimes ulcerate. This inflammation of the esophagus is called esophagitis.

Severe esophagitis can lead to damage and ultimate scarring of the esophagus. Scarring can occur at the junction between the esophagus and stomach, and a narrowing or stricture may result. If a stricture is present, food may start sticking in the esophagus -- or even completely lodge there. This is called an esophageal food impaction, which is scary and far from fun. I've gone to the ER on many occasions to endoscopically remove various impacted food items.

The most common item that lodges in the esophagus is meat. If a piece of meat lodges there, it can be very painful. You can't swallow your own saliva, because your esophagus is blocked. Contrary to popular belief, you can breathe just fine -- your trachea (windpipe) is a separate tube and remains open to allow for air passage. Over the years I've endoscopically removed the equivalent of an entire buffet of steak, pork, chicken, pastrami, and carne asada from the esophagus. Most foods can be gently advanced into the stomach with the help of the endoscope, or gently pulled back out.

Some people feel the sensation of food getting stuck in the esophagus but continue eating, hoping that the additional food will push the stuck food into the stomach. *Hello* -- please don't do this. On more than one occasion I've encountered a four-course meal in the esophagus and spent hours pulling out peas, carrots, bread, salad, and some vaguely identifiable meat substance.

My most recent experience was a 55-year-old woman who for years had difficulty swallowing. She'd never shared her problem with anyone and landed in the ER when her Chinese lunch stopped short of her stomach. I discovered semi-chewed broccoli, snow peas, carrots, and an unpleasant chicken-like substance stuck in her lower esophagus. I successfully advanced her lunch past a tight esophageal stricture and into the stomach. I then dilated the stricture using a small balloon that was passed through an endoscope. She recovered quickly, but I can assure you that Chinese food was not on my menu for months following that particular episode.

GI doctors encounter many other interesting items that people somehow manage to swallow. I've encountered pens, pencils, coins, tin foil, safety pins, balls of hair (this hobby is no longer reserved for the feline family), marbles, paper clips, and toothpicks lodged in the esophagus or stomach. One young girl's stomach looked like she'd swallowed a whole shelf of items from the local office supply store.

Early on in my medical career I was summoned to a local emergency room at two in the morning to extract a foreign body from the esophagus of a newly married bride – still sporting her lovely white wedding dress. Could it be an impaction of chicken, beef, or a favorite item from the buffet line? Not this time! It seems that during the obligatory cake-in-your-face rite, her inebriated groom failed to look at the piece of cake he jammed into his lovely new bride's mouth – with the unfortunate result that the plastic good-luck horseshoe from the top of the wedding cake was immediately transferred into the bride's esophagus.

In order to safely sedate her for an endoscopic extraction, I enlisted the help of an anesthesiologist who administered general anesthesia while I gently lassoed and removed the horseshoe from her esophagus. The scariest part of this whole event was that the cardiothoracic surgeons were on standby -- because if I didn't succeed she'd need open-chest surgery to remove the foreign body. When I finished I placed the horseshoe in a plastic bag and left it next to her in the recovery room.

The groom was a military man who was leaving for the Middle East the next day. He took the horseshoe with him for good luck.

There are many factors involved with reflux and the consequent esophageal damage. Alcohol and tobacco use are frequent factors, but the biggest contributing factor I see in my practice is the poor food choices that so often lead to obesity. When you're overweight, those extra pounds put extra pressure on your stomach and diaphragm. I've seen hundreds of my patients suffer from worsening heartburn as their weight increased. I began to realize that if I didn't find a way to address their underlying dietary and weight issues, they'd probably require lifelong reflux medications. This reality also concerned me from the standpoint of their overall state of health.

In many people who achieve effective weight loss, heartburn symptoms are decreased significantly or eliminated completely. It's not clear to me whether that's because pounds are melting away or because they've changed their diets and lifestyles. Most likely it's a combination of these factors.

Here are some **lifestyle** guidelines for addressing reflux:

- Try to eat small, frequent meals instead of three big meals a day. Small amounts of food mean less workload for the stomach and therefore allow for better digestive capacity and improved gastric emptying.

- Avoid high-fat meals such as those from the fast-food chains. Fast food is more likely to precipitate a reflux attack. High-fat foods will remain in the stomach longer and predispose to more regurgitation.
- Don't overeat. This will lead to gastric distention and interfere with the stomach's ability to empty properly.
- Don't wear tight clothing around the abdomen.
- Eat slowly and chew foods thoroughly.
- Avoid or significantly limit sodas, alcohol, chocolate, and caffeinated beverages.
- Eliminate cigarette smoking and chewing tobacco.
- Avoid NSAIDS (aspirin, Motrin, Advil, etc).
- Maintain upright position during and at least one to two hours after eating.
- Try elevating the head of the bed six to eight inches when lying down.
- If you take an antacid, avoid those with aluminum, which is a toxic substance.
- If food starts to stick in the esophagus, see a GI doctor **immediately**.

One of my patients told me he had the best cure for heartburn and gave me this story:

A man goes to the doctor with a long history of indigestion and acid reflux. When the doctor gets his history and gives him the physical, he discovers the poor guy has tried practically every therapy known to man for his digestive problems, with little to no relief.

"Listen," says the doc, "I have severe reflux too and the advice I'm going to give you isn't anything I learned in medical school – it comes from my own experience. When I have severe digestive problems, I go home, get in a nice hot bathtub, and soak for a while. Then I have my wife sponge me off with the hottest water I can stand, especially around the fore-head and upper abdomen. This helps a little. Then I get out of the tub, take her into the bedroom, and make passionate love to her. I think you should give this a try, and come back and see me in six weeks."

Six weeks later, the patient returned with a big grin. "Doc! I took your advice and it works. It really works! I've had reflux for seventeen years, and this is the first time anyone has ever helped me."

"Well," says the doctor, "I'm glad I could help."

"By the way, Doc," the patient adds, "You have a REALLY nice house."

-- Anonymous

CHAPTER 7

OBESITY: NOT A LAUGHING MATTER

"How disgusting is this? Here it is folks, this is the end of the world....A restaurant in Decatur, Georgia, is now serving a double bacon cheeseburger that's served between two Krispy Kreme doughnuts. We're now officially ancient Rome. This is the end of our civilization as we know it. In fact, they don't know how many calories are in this thing because nobody can count that high."

-- Jay Leno

It comes as no surprise that obesity is epidemic in this country -- just look around. The scale in my office measures up to 250 pounds, and during every clinic at least one or two patients refuse to step on the scale because their weight exceeds its limit. I see the fatigue and desperation in their eyes and I'm shocked at how many medications they're on. There seems to be a very direct and consistent correlation between how overweight the person is and how many medications they're on, and today's food and pharmaceutical industries help perpetuate this terrible trend.

"Pringles is coming out with a new wider can. Their slogan will be, 'From our wide can to yours.'"

-- Jay Leno

My patients suffer with multiple digestive problems stemming from all of the nutritionally bankrupt foods they're consuming, not to mention the digestive issues resulting from the myriad of medications they're on. Medications are some of the worst offenders when it comes to altering the natural function of your digestive tract. And the more overweight you are, the greater chance you'll end up on more and more prescriptions. It is a vicious cycle that unfortunately has become the American way. One of my patients who suffered from obesity brought me a "guide to the American diet."

1. Introduce as many toxic foods as possible. Suggestions include potato chips, pizza with extra cheese, white bread, milk, coffee or coke, milkshakes from edible oil products, fried chicken, potatoes deep-fried in beef fat, eggs from chemically-raised chickens, steak with extra barbecue sauce, and a small portion of pesticide-laden mineral-depleted vegetables. Throw in a couple of chocolate bars to insure an optimum toxin level.

2. Eat very few raw fruits and vegetables. If you must eat vegetables, make sure the life has been cooked out of them. The best fruits are canned and preserved in sugar syrup.

3. Give your juice machine away. Drink bottled or canned juices with artificial flavors and food colorings. Canned vegetable juice is fine because all the enzymes have been destroyed through pasteurization.

4. Swallow food whole. Use butter as a lubricant. Deep- fried foods will require less chewing.

5. Eat as much as you possibly can at one sitting. This conditions the muscles that support the stomach to expand, accommodating an increased volume of food.

6. Avoid fiber at all cost. If forced to eat whole wheat flour, pick the bits of bran from the bread. This will allow the food to pass more slowly through the intestine so the body may absorb maximum toxic chemicals.

7. Do not exercise. Exercise oxygenates the cells and triggers the lymphatic system that cleans the body. Try to remain in an inactive horizontal position.

8. Snack regularly during the night so as to curb the body's natural tendency to detoxify during sleep.

<u>Statistics now reveal that 81% of our population is overweight. We are in crisis: we are literally eating ourselves to death.</u>

The data from the 1999 - 2000 National Health and Nutrition Examination Survey is considered to be one of the better assessments of American's weight because of the length and size of the study. These numbers continue to escalate at an alarming rate. The statistics revealed that:

- 31%, or about 59 million adults over 20, are *obese*. "Obese" is defined as 30 or more pounds over healthy body weight; "overweight" as 10 to 30 pounds above a healthy weight.
- 33% of adult women are obese, compared with 28% of men.
- 50% of black women are obese compared with 40% of Mexican-American women and 30% of white women. (The survey doesn't have a category for all Hispanics.) There is virtually no difference in obesity among men based on race.
- 5% of people overall were extremely obese. That's up from about 3% in the early 1990s.
- Approximately *18 million* children are obese.

This current obesity trend is hitting a critical level with our children. Obesity and type II diabetes are now the two most alarming epidemics facing our children. The U.S. Center for Disease Control (CDC) predicts that children born in 2000 and beyond face an alarming one in three chance of developing type II diabetes. A child with type II diabetes could lose as much as 27 years off his or her life span. This data was presented by the CDC at the American Diabetes Association's 63rd conference.

Type II diabetes is lifestyle-related and preventable, and we should all be addressing its prevention or reversal in adults as well as children. It's a debilitating, terrible disease that can predispose to blindness, loss of limbs, multiple vascular problems, kidney failure, and death.

According to the *Journal of the American Medical Association*, obesity, lack of physical activity, and the consequent associated illnesses are overtaking tobacco as the leading cause of *preventable death* in this country. In 2000, obesity and inactivity caused 400,000 deaths, more than 16% of all deaths. In the same year, tobacco-related deaths were 18.1%. Obesity cost America $117 billion in 2000, according to the surgeon general. For the first time in history we're actually witnessing a decline in the American lifespan. Obesity has been linked to several serious medical conditions, including:

- Heart disease and stroke
- Type II diabetes
- High blood pressure
- Osteoarthritis
- Gallbladder dysfunction and gallstones
- Sleep apnea
- High cholesterol
- Chronic back pain

- Bladder-control problems such as stress incontinence
- Complications of pregnancy
- Severe depression
- Cancer (uterine, cervical, ovarian, breast, liver, multiple myeloma, non-hodgkin's lymphoma, pancreatic, colon and prostate)

A major study from the American Cancer Society offers the most compelling evidence to date that being overweight may significantly increase your risk of dying from cancer. Researchers suggest that approximately 90,000 cancer deaths may be related to obesity and therefore preventable. For almost all cancers, the risk of death increased as did excess body mass. For the heaviest men and women, the risk of dying from cancer exceeded 50%.

We're also learning that exercise alone will not reduce the associated health risks that stem from excess weight. The *New England Journal of Medicine* looked at this issue and found that women who were physically active but obese had almost twice the risk of death than women who were both active and lean.

"There are now more overweight people in America than average-weight people. So overweight people are now average. Which means you've met your New Year's resolution."

-- Jay Leno

If excess fat is carried in the abdominal area, this "visceral" fat poses an even higher risk of heart disease, cancer, and diabetes. This fat deposition is a ball of toxic waste, a problem that can be addressed by supporting our body's natural cleansing abilities. The following studies are truly revealing.

Since 1976, the Environmental Protection Agency has been engaged in the National Human Adipose Tissue Survey (NHATS). This is a fascinating look at what our fat cells hold on to. In this study, adipose (fat) samples were taken from cadavers and elective surgeries from all regions of the country and the levels of toxins measured. In 1982, NHATS expanded beyond its original list to look for the presence of 54 different environmental chemical toxins. The results are cause for great concern:

Five of the chemicals--OCDD (a dioxin), styrene, 1,4-dichlorobenzene, xylene, and ethyl phenol--were found in 100% of all samples. Another nine chemicals--benzene, toluene, chlorobenzene, ethyl benzene, DDE, three dioxins, and one furan--were found in 91-98% of all samples. In addition, polychlorinated biphenols (PCBs) were found in 83% of all samples and beta-*BHC* in 87%. The bottom line to all of these findings is that a total of 20 toxic compounds were found in 76% or more of all samples. These ongoing assessments have shown quite clearly that it's not a question of whether we're carrying a burden of toxic compounds, but how much and how they adversely affect our health. Knowing the degree of illness and disease in this country, it's obvious what these compounds are doing to our cells and vital organs -- and ultimately our overall health.

Additional research has shown the same alarming facts. A CDC study of 5,994 subjects aged 12-74 found that 99.5% had p,p-DDE at significant levels. A study of adipose levels of chemicals in cadavers from Texas showed the presence of p,p-DDE, dieldrin, oxychlordane, heptachlor epoxide, and para-BHC in 100% of all samples. A study of 4-year-olds in Michigan showed the presence of DDT in over 70%, PCB in 50%, and PBB in 13-21%. Nursing was the primary source of exposure for these children. Many toxins have been found in breast milk, directly passed to the baby. All of this information is eye-opening, frightening, and should not be ignored. Denial is not an acceptable option.

These studies demonstrate the fact that fat cells carry a lot of toxins. And although mainstream medicine doesn't support cleansing the body as a way to lose weight, it's very logical and makes perfect sense to me. When the body is fueled by the right nutrients and the digestive system and liver are functioning optimally, the body is able to flush accumulated toxins. I've witnessed countless people who successfully removed a significant amount of accumulated visceral fat through safe, effective cleansing. It's an amazing process that's now supported by substantial research.

Cleansing and refueling the body is what I like to call the "anti-diet" approach to optimal health and weight management. "Diets" are often imbalanced and don't address the underlying issue of strengthening the immune system and ridding the body of toxins. I've never recommended a "typical" fad diet in twelve years of medicine. Diets often rob the body of essential nutrients, and although the scale may temporarily impress you, when you go back to your normal routine you become a fatter, more toxic version of your former self. Is it any wonder why people "yo-yo" diet and experience a frustrating 98% failure rate long-term? Why not embrace a program that gives your body the right nutrients, the right balance, and the ability to once and for all win the battle of the bulge?

"The second day of a diet is always easier than the first. By the second day you're off it."

-- Jackie Gleanson

Chapter 8

CONSTIPATION ALLEVIATION

A man went to the doctor complaining of terrible constipation. The doctor examined him and gave him a prescription for some tablets to be taken right before bedtime. Two weeks later the patient returned for a check-up and the doctor asked him how his constipation was. The doctor was puzzled when the man gloomily answered that the pills worked fine and that he had a large bowel movement every morning at six am.

"So why the long face?" asked the doctor.

"Because I don't get up until seven."

-- Anonymous

Having regular constipation can lead to serious illness. Fecal matter should move through your colon easily and in an appropriate time frame. When feces remain in your colon too long, it becomes toxic. This toxicity can spread into every part of the body.

Over 90 years ago and more, doctors knew about the importance of a clean colon. In 1908 Eli Metchnifoff, director of the Pasteur Institute, was awarded the Nobel Prize for Medicine. His research showed that pathogenic (bad) colon bacteria produced toxic secretions and by-products, which acted as slow poisoning of the entire body.

Metchnifoff believed that toxic matter retained in the colon was responsible for virtually every degenerative disease. In fact, his belief was so strong that he suggested man's life span might be actually cut in half when his colon was neglected and allowed to have excessive toxic-producing bacteria.

The function of the colon in our bodies could be compared to a sewer system in a large city. Just envision what would happen if the sewers in your area became clogged by excessive waste. Within a short time the whole neighborhood would be running with filth and an unbearable stench. Now think of the process that occurs in our bodies when we're constipated. When the large intestine is congested with stagnant waste, poisons back up into the system and pollute the inner environment. This has been labeled by some health care professionals as autointoxication or self-poisoning.

In my practice I see an over-abundance of constipated patients, including ones whose bowels move as infrequently as once every two to four weeks. Just imagine the toxins that are building up in your body when this occurs. The sluggish intestine will often cause serious systemic symptoms that plague the individual on a daily basis.

Many of my constipated patients suffer from the following problems - all of which appear to be the effect of auto-intoxication.

- Bad breath and foul-smelling gas
- Frequent infections: colds, viruses
- Frequent headaches for no apparent reason
- General migrating aches and pains
- Multiple food sensitivities and allergies
- Low energy, loss of vitality for no apparent reason
- Lower back pain
- Sleep disturbances
- Depression and irritability
- Inability to concentrate
- Premenstrual syndrome (PMS)
- Vaginal yeast infections
- Nonspecific skin rashes and acne
- Low grade fevers

Many health professionals agree that every cell and vital organ of our body is affected by significant constipation. Constipation causes us to feel irritable and depressed. We also feel weak, bloated, tired, and uncomfortable. Constipation can lead to chronic hemorrhoidal problems manifesting into hemorrhoidal bleeding.

Our modern lifestyle has taken its toll on our digestive/elimination organs. Refined, processed, low-fiber foods, animal fats, lack of exercise, dehydration, and an ever-increasing level of stress all contribute to sluggish elimination. The incidence of diverticulosis has increased dramatically over the last 40 years. Diverticulosis is a weakening of the colon wall, allowing saccular pockets to develop. These pockets can harbor bacteria and cause a severe and often painful condition called diverticulitis. The first step in everyone's health program should be stimulating and toning all the elimination organs, and the colon is the best place to begin.

A diet with enough fiber (25 to 35 grams daily) helps form a soft bulky stool. It's important to increase fiber slowly, since rapid increases in fiber can cause gas and discomfort. High-fiber foods include pinto beans, whole grains and bran cereals, fresh fruits, and vegetables such as asparagus, brussel sprouts, cabbage, and carrots. I also recommend prunes and figs. Oatmeal, applesauce, legumes, and barley help to soften the stool. Flax seed is an excellent source of fiber and delivers the full benefit of Omega 3, 6 and 9 essential fatty acids. For people prone to constipation, limiting foods that have little or no fiber such as ice cream, cheese, meat, and processed and fast foods is also important.

Other changes that can help treat and prevent constipation include staying very well hydrated with at least two liters of water daily, engaging in daily exercise to increase intestinal tone, and reserving enough time to have a good bowel movement. The urge to have a bowel movement should not be ignored. Relaxation techniques, breathing exercises, yoga, and biofeedback can assist with constipation that's associated with stress. Avoid caffeine, tobacco, and other stimulant compounds that will eventually interfere with the intestine's natural ability to produce regular contractions and elimination.

Avoid drugs that have a constipating effect. Narcotic pain relievers are some of the worst offenders.

Magnesium is beneficial in many areas of the body and is a very important mineral when it comes to addressing constipation. Supplemental magnesium allows for better water regulation in the colon and helps to promote better intestinal motility. Vitamin C has a gentle non-addicting laxative effect. And the lubricating effects of the inner heart of the aloe vera plant can also help gently assist intestinal elimination.

Normal frequency of bowel movements differs among individuals. An adequately functioning bowel will eliminate 1 - 4 times daily and should not involve undue straining. It's also a good idea to look at each bowel movement to check for general color and appearance. A drastic change in shape of the stools or the appearance of blood (red or black tarry stools) can signal a serious intestinal problem.

Chapter 9 ———————————

HAVE YOUR
COLON EVALUATED

A man came in to St Joe's Hospital for colon-cancer surgery. The operation went well, and as the groggy patient regained consciousness, a Sister of Mercy nun waiting by his bed reassured him.

"Mr. Smith, you're going to be just fine," she said as she patted his hand. "We do need to know however, how do you intend to pay for your stay here? Are you covered by insurance?"

"No, I'm not," the man whispered hoarsely.

"Can you pay in cash?"

"I'm afraid I can't, Sister."

"Do you have any close relatives, then?"

"Just my sister in New Mexico," he said, "but she's a spinster nun."

"Nuns aren't spinsters, Mr. Smith. They're married to God."

"Okay," the man said with a smile. "Then bill my brother-in-law."

- Anonymous

Colon cancer begins in the large intestine (the colon). Rectal cancer begins in the rectum, the part of the large intestine closest to the anus (the outside opening to the intestine). These forms of cancer have many common features and are sometimes referred to together as colorectal cancer (CRC).

CRC is the second leading cause of cancer death in the U.S., and unfortunately I've diagnosed many people with this highly preventable disease. In nonsmokers, CRC is the number-one cause of cancer-related mortality. CRC can sneak up on you, and in 2004 it was estimated that approximately 60,000 deaths resulted from it. Yet if proper screening evaluations are performed, colon cancer can be prevented in the large majority of people.

The American Cancer Society recommends that if you don't have significant risk factors for the development of CRC, your first screening colonoscopy should take place at age 50. Because this procedure is often misunderstood, many people avoid having a colonoscopy because this prospect scares them. But a colonoscopy may save your life and is an easy procedure that simply requires a "colon cleanse" the day before your test.

Adequate visualization of the large intestine is the key to a successful colonoscopy. The colon needs to be clean in order for the GI doctor to introduce a small flexible tube into the rectum and visualize the entire large intestine. Conscious sedation that induces a dream-like state is administered during the procedure, resulting in a comfortable experience most people have absolutely no recollection of. A comfortably sedated patient ensures a safer exam -- GI doctors don't want their patients flipping around on the table like a carp.

Most colorectal cancers begin as a polyp, which usually starts as a harmless growth in the wall of the colon. However, as a polyp gets larger, it can develop into a cancer that grows and spreads. One of the goals during a screening colonoscopy is to identify polyps and remove them so that colon cancer can be prevented. Countless lives have been saved through screening colonoscopies.

A colonoscopy should be performed at an earlier age than 50 if warning signs are present or if a family history exists. Don't ignore your body when it's trying to tell you something. The following symptoms warrant further or often immediate evaluation:

- Bleeding from your rectum
- Blood in your stool or in the toilet after you have a bowel movement
- A change in the shape of your stool
- Cramping pain in your mid or lower abdomen
- A feeling of discomfort or an urge to have a bowel movement when there's no need to have one.

You should also begin colon-cancer screening at a younger age if any of the following are true about you:

- You had colorectal cancer or large polyps in the past
- You have a close relative (brother, sister, parent, or child) who has had colorectal cancer before age 60
- You have ulcerative colitis or Crohn's disease

- You have a hereditary colon cancer syndrome

If you're in one of these groups, you may need to be tested more often than a person who doesn't have risk factors for colorectal cancer.

Although it remains unclear why so many people develop polyps or colon cancer, diet appears to be associated with colorectal cancer risk. Genetics also plays a significant role, though many people without a family history are diagnosed with colorectal cancer.

Among populations that consume a diet high in fat, calories, alcohol, and meat and low in calcium and folate, colorectal cancer is more likely to develop than among populations that consume a low-fat, high-fiber diet. A diet low in vitamin D may also increase the risk of colorectal cancer. A diet high in saturated fat combined with a sedentary lifestyle may increase the risk of colorectal cancer, and there's also evidence that smoking may be associated with an increased risk. According to a recent study from the Dartmouth Medical School, taking calcium supplements protects against the development of colon polyps, and this benefit appears to persist for up to 5 years after people stop taking the supplements.

Prevention is the best medicine, and appropriate screening for colorectal cancer could save your life. Over the years, patients who have undergone colonoscopy procedures manage to make me smile with classic comments regarding their exam. My favorite line was from an older gentleman who said to me in recovery, ***"I'm so glad I got this out of the*** *way. But will you write me a note for my wife, saying that my head is not, in fact, up there?"*

Chapter 10

CLEANSING AND NUTRITIONAL REPLACEMENT: A SIGNIFICANT PIECE OF THE PUZZLE

A BRIEF HISTORY OF MEDICINE

I have a stomach ache:

2000 B.C. –   *Here, eat this root.*

1000 A.D. –   *That root is heathen, say this prayer.*

1850 A.D. –   *That prayer is superstition, drink this potion.*

1940 A.D. –   *That potion is snake oil, swallow this pill.*

1985 A.D. –   *That pill is ineffective, take this antibiotic.*

2000 A.D. -   *That antibiotic is artificial. Here, eat this root.*

-- Anonymous

I've presented a range of medical issues facing our world today. While no one product or program can single-handedly remedy these problems, it's imperative that you do something to improve and support your own health. The information I'm providing is educational and in some instances includes my opinions and conclusions. I'm not making an attempt to formally prescribe treatment, and any nutritional or exercise program should be discussed with your personal licensed health professional.

> *Let thy food be thy medicine and thy medicine be thy food.*
>
> *-- Hippocrates (460-377 B.C.)*

The approach to wellness is coming full circle. In my quest to uncover and qualify available natural alternatives for achieving optimal health, I've discovered certain high-quality nutrients that support our body's natural ability to detoxify. During my medical career I've always felt that one of the most important missing links in western medicine is a consistent approach to internal cleansing.

For years I studied the detrimental effects of toxins on the body, so I was intrigued with various herbal supplements and organic nutrients that assist the body in achieving cleansing and replenishing. I also understood that most Americans were overfed and yet nutritionally undernourished, so I was very interested in multiple high-quality nutrients that could be synergistically blended and used together as meal replacements. Unique food technologies are now available and offer a fresh approach for people to recapture many aspects of their health including substantial, safe, documented weight loss.

CHAPTER 10

For many individuals, weight loss is obviously important. But remember, everything you put into your mouth has an impact on your *overall* health including the health of your liver and digestive system. Well-rounded nutritional programs should provide amino acids to increase energy, support the immune system, and help mental focus. Meal replacement protein shakes should contain a balance of protein, fat, and carbohydrates to enhance metabolism and assist with weight management. Herbs and a complete range of vitamins can be used to help the body cleanse and internally strengthen. Trace minerals are also important to aid the digestive tract in optimum absorption of nutrients. Health and vitality are nature's greatest gifts. Here are various supplements, herbs and vitamins that can help you and your family design a program for a healthier lifestyle.

Pharmaceutical Grade Organic Whey Protein. True organic whey protein is antibiotic-, steroid- and hormone-free. It's a rich source of branched- chain amino acids and essential amino acids that are critically important for anyone who engages in exercise, sports, or resistance training. Whey protein in highly supportive of the immune system, and whey concentrates contain the immunoglobulin IgA, which protects your intestines by binding with harmful bacteria. Whey protein comes from cow's milk and is acceptable for any vegetarian diet that allows for dairy, including lacto-ovo, lacto, and ovo types of vegetarian diets.

Antioxidants. Toxic compounds are responsible for the development of free radicals, which are highly reactive and have the potential to damage cellular DNA, thus leading to cancer, a weakened immune system, and accelerated aging. Antioxidants are substances that block the chemical reactions that generate free radicals and can help destroy already formed ones. Various antioxidants include vitamin E, vitamin C, vitamin A, selenium, and carotenoids, which are found in yellow and orange fruits and vegetables or in supplements containing alpha- and beta-catotene, lycopene, and lutein. Some of the best antioxidant supplements also contain coenzyme Q and extracts of green tea, milk thistle, bilberry, grape seed, red raspberry, and pomegranate. Ingesting antioxidants can help support the immune system, retard aging, and offer protection against cancer.

Digestive Enzymes. Digestive enzymes assist with the small intestine's ability to absorb and utilize essential nutrients. The best digestive enzyme complexes are developed to work in all pH environments in the upper intestinal tract. Digestive enzymes are very important in people who suffer from pancreatic insufficiency.

Aloe vera juice from the heart of the aloe plant. Because of the way the aloe is harvested, this liquid is quite hypoallergenic and will not promote diarrhea. Many of my IBS (Irritable Bowel Syndrome) patients have told me that if they drink pure aloe juice they notice less gas and bloating. I have several patients that cut down the aloe plants from their own yards, scoop out the inner portion, and mix it with water. It can be bitter, but several of my IBS patients can't go without it. Dr. Andrew Weil, considered one of the world's leading authorities on natural therapies, recommends pure aloe vera as one of the natural treatments for ulcerative colitis and Crohn's disease.

Cleansing Herbs. Herbs such as suma, peppermint, fennel seed, and licorice have been used in many cultures to support and aid in digestion. Peppermint is a wonderful digestive remedy that can provide relief from gas, bloating, nausea, and gastric upset. Peppermint has a calming effect on the smooth muscle of the intestinal tract and is felt to promote the flow of bile from the gallbladder into the small bowel, thus aiding in the digestion of fats. Fennel seed is found on many dinner tables in India because it's taken regularly as a digestive aid to help with bloating and gas. Licorice has been used to help protect the lining of the stomach, and suma to soothe the digestive tract.

Adaptogens. Adaptogens were classified by the ancient Chinese as "superior plants" and are unique among nutrients. More than a thousand scientific publications from the U.S., China, Japan, and the Soviet Union have been published in international and American scientific journals in recent years about the multiple benefits of Adaptogens. In herbal medicine, Adaptogens are used to help the body "adapt" to imbalances that stress the body externally or internally. Adaptogens assist in the body's self-regulatory systems. Adaptogenic substances include Ashwaghanda extract, Shizandra extract, Siberian ginseng, Siberian golden root extract, maca extract, wolfberry extract and Nepali Shilajit extract. Recent research from Germany has shown that Adaptogens improve the performance of the immune system by up to three times.

Minerals and trace minerals. Ionic (charged) minerals are the best form for absorption into our body. Minerals are the key to enzyme activation in the digestive tract. When minerals are present, our intestines allow for ultimate absorption of vitamins and essential nutrients. Enzymes help the body break down nutrients into an absorbable form. By flooding your body with ionic minerals, not only will the digestive tract come alive, so will other key systems in your body. Magnesium is a very important mineral that is supportive of adequate colon function. Magnesium provides fuel for our cells and assists with improved waste elimination.

Lipotropic nutrients. In naturopathic medicine lipotropics are used to assist the removal of fat from the liver. Lipotropic agents include methionine, choline, betaine, folic acid, and vitamin B12. Many of these nutrients have been used for years to support improved liver function.

Lactobacillus and Acidophilus. These are probiotics that provide balance to your intestinal tract. Probiotics are friendly bacteria that secrete substances to kill harmful pathogenic bacteria and create a balanced intestinal environment. Antibiotics, steroids, birth control pills, poor diet, and chronic constipation can upset the normal equilibrium of the intestines. Probiotics help to create a favorable environment, thus protecting the intestinal tract and the rest of the body from harmful bacterial endotoxins.

Soluble fiber and stabilized flax seed. It goes without saying that eating more fiber is a consistent recommendation by GI doctors across the country. Increased fiber acts like a cleansing "broom" in the colon and can help improve intestinal peristalsis (contractility and movement) to allow for better elimination of waste. Fiber helps to prevent an irritable bowel, diverticulosis, and possibly colon cancer. Flax seed delivers the full benefits of Omega 3, 6 and 9 essential fatty acids plus fiber, protein, vitamins, minerals, and amino acids that are important nutrients for the digestive tract and overall good health. The U.S. surgeon general recommends a daily ingestion of 20-35 grams of fiber a day.

Apple Cider Vinegar. This ingredient has been used by many cultures to promote better digestion. It's an antioxidant that has antibacterial properties and provides potassium for the body. You need normal potassium levels in the bloodstream to promote adequate intestinal peristalsis.

Pau d'arco. This compound is harvested from the inner bark of the *Tabebuia avellanedae* tree, which is native to Brazil. Pau d'arco has been used in many cultures traditionally to treat a wide range of conditions including arthritis, inflammation of the prostate gland (prostatitis), dysentery, and ulcers. Preliminary laboratory research examining the properties of pau d'arco is beginning to suggest that the traditional uses may have scientific merit. Many herbalists recommend it to help with candida (yeast) overgrowth of the vaginal and intestinal areas. More and more information is coming to light about the adverse effects of yeast on our intestinal tracts. It is felt that yeast overgrowth can cause significant gas and alternation in bowel patterns and cause a predisposition to various food allergies or sensitivities. Candida may also play a significant role in the difficulties some people experience when trying to lose weight.

Cinnamon. With its sweet and spicy flavor, cinnamon has been used by many different cultures for its medicinal properties -- for hundreds, even thousands, of years. Cinnamon is a rich source of magnesium, which is helpful for the irritable bowel and for people dealing with constipation. Cinnamon aids in digestion, and research is now showing its benefits for diabetes.

Many of these nutrients are supportive of the liver and as I've said, the liver is vital to the entire digestive process. By supporting this incredible detoxifying organ, your body can better utilize absorbed proteins and fats. The liver will take those needed amino acids and convert them into healthy brain chemicals. If your brain chemistry is in balance, you start to make better lifestyle choices. What I've noticed in my patients and family is that when the body is in nutritional balance, many unhealthy cravings go away. An underlying principle I've used for years and found to make perfect sense is this: "THE HEALTHY BODY CRAVES HEALTHY

THINGS, AND THE UNHEALTHY BODY CRAVES UN-
HEALTHY THINGS."

My mother-in-law lost her craving for cigarettes after she began a nutritional program that supported her liver and digestive system. She started exercising and drinking more water, and she introduced organic nutrients into her diet. She stopped smoking, a habit of over 30 years. She shed excess body fat and had more energy. Once off the cigarettes she noticed that her indigestion disappeared and her taste buds came alive. She looks and feels better than ever.

A business associate of mine spent most of his adult life drinking an average of three pots of coffee per day. He suffered from indigestion and was overweight. He started on a nutritional cleansing program that supported his liver and digestive system. After dropping over fifteen pounds and several inches around his waist in the first two weeks, he also noticed he'd lost all cravings for coffee. He calculated he's saving $242.00 a month due to his renewed health and his digestive system is performing optimally.

Many options are available when introducing your body to a well-rounded, safe nutritional program. The program should address cleansing and nourishing the body, not starving it. Exercise, eating well, and hydration are key components of any health-oriented program. The nutritional system my family and I have used for two and a half years and one I highly recommend is called Isagenix. The Isagenix system is a unique food technology that addresses cleansing and revitalization of the internal body and contains high-quality ingredients that are highly supportive of the liver and digestive system. It's a meal replacement system, and you select the program that best fits with your individual goals and lifestyle. Certain programs were developed for significant weight loss and other programs offer a simple maintenance plan to complement an on-going healthy lifestyle.

Embracing and committing to a healthy lifestyle is the key to success. Unlike most drugs, this type of approach is not a band-aid, and some type of daily maintenance is vitally important. Based on your health and weight management goals, the perfect way to give your body balance is to commit to an ongoing daily nutrition and exercise plan. This type of commitment is appropriate for the entire family.

A good friend of mine started a structured nutritional and exercise program, lost forty pounds in six weeks, looked and felt great. Intestinal issues that plagued him for years were gone. He was exercising regularly and found himself drinking much less alcohol. He told me he felt more mentally alert and that his cravings for junk food had disappeared. He stuck with a maintenance program and continues to look and feel incredible.

I had the chance to ask his wife what she liked best about what had happened to her husband. To my surprise she told me, "He's nice again. He's calm at work, and all of his employees are commenting on his relaxed attitude. He doesn't complain about his stomach any more, and he smiles all the time."

My family's and my personal results, along with the growing number of life-changing results I've witnessed in countless others, have compelled me to introduce the concept of internal cleansing and replenishment to nearly every person who enters my life. Truly this is what health care -- not sick care -- is all about. But unfortunately, in the traditional medical world, nutritional or alternative approaches are often met with unhealthy criticism. After all, in medical school, students are taught a tremendous amount about prescribing pharmaceuticals and very little about nutritional physiology and environmental toxicity. A nurse once asked me if endorsing cleansing and nutritional programs was medically ethical. I told her that after discovering this amazing approach to health and wellness, it would be unethical for me not to share this option with everyone.

Take this with you:

If you could look into the future and picture the perfect health scenario, what would that be? Now, without any if's, and's, or but's, set a plan into action. Always remember: if you don't know where you're going, then you're already there.

The statements contained in this chapter have not been evaluated by the Food and Drug Administration and are not intended to diagnose, treat, cure, or prevent any disease. Always consult your personal healthcare professional before starting this or any weight management or exercise program.

Conclusion:

AN EMERGING TRILLION-DOLLAR INDUSTRY

By Dan Maes

"Take care of your body. It is the only place you have to live."

-- Jim Rohn

Through experience I've gained during twelve years of involvement in nutrition, wellness, and health education, I firmly believe that in most cases we all possess the ability to take control of and manage our own health. Historically, our incredible bodies assumed this role and for the most part the process was on auto-pilot. This has always been one of the great miracles of life.

Over time, however, as we've continued to pollute and damage our environment -- including the once fertile soil so essential to the development of our natural food sources -- our body's ability to perform its own miracle has been greatly challenged. Although most American adults can't be completely exonerated, we're not entirely to blame for the deterioration of our personal state of health. Unbeknownst to most of us, a prevalent tyranny has slowly but surely been driving

America's state of health into the ground. This tyranny is largely responsible for America's health crisis.

Today in this country literally billions of our hard-earned dollars are being poured into the pockets of the powerful and controversial food and pharmaceutical industries. Am I against research and development of life-enhancing and life-saving drugs? Absolutely not! Am I against the production of high quality, convenient foods that support our growing economy? Absolutely not! What concerns me is the greed that has enveloped these trillion-dollar industries, perpetuating the deterioration of our health and accelerating America's health crisis.

There's a difference between making it convenient for us to find and consume food that complements our busy lifestyles and knowingly lacing our conveniently packaged food and abundant fast food products with carcinogens and addictive ingredients. There's a difference between the necessary recommendation of pharmaceuticals for transient or emergent care and the commercialization, glamorization, and careless over-marketing of them – which can only lead to their being over-prescribed.

Much like what the food industry has done for so many years, the pharmaceutical industry has recently broadened its advertising strategy to target unsuspecting people who watch television, listen to the radio, read magazines, pick up pamphlets in doctors' offices, etc. The health care industry, including the pharmaceutical companies, no longer caters to just health care professionals but now bombards the American public -- including our children -- with its messages, hyped and dangerously alluring. There are even TV ads for drugs that don't tell the viewer what condition the drug is intended to address! ("Ask your doctor if XYZ is right for you.")

Remember the good old days when it was okay to forget something once in a while or wander from thought to thought while in the middle of a conversation without being lured into taking medication for a condition called AADD (adult attention deficit disorder?") Remember when your child periodically acted up in school without your being influenced by pharmaceutical company ads into asking your doctor for drugs to cure him or her of ADHD? Remember when men could actually turn on the television or read a magazine without being swayed into thinking they were sexually inadequate and needed drugs for erectile dysfunction? Remember when people didn't rush to take a purple pill for acid reflux disease if they experienced stomach discomfort after wolfing down two pounds of ribs and a plate of greasy French fries? Wow! And you used to think you were just too tired to have sex, had a wandering mind, or an occasional bout of heartburn.

The food and drug industries have become so big and powerful that they've literally created their own self-contained economies, with seemingly no end in sight. The primary beneficiaries of this staggering growth trend are the shareholders and the high-level executives who sit atop the corporate pyramids that are driving these industries. The unfortunate victims are the innocent consumers who fall into the trap of believing that these industries may actually have their best interests in mind. Greedy media conglomerates, largely funded by these very industries, exacerbate the problem through the proliferation of suspect and misleading advertising messages. This has become a vicious cycle and is one of the driving forces behind America's health crisis. I recommend that anyone interested in learning more about these topics watch the eye-opening movie "*Super Size Me*" and reading the book "*Fast Food Nation*".

On a more positive note, there is a rapidly evolving $200 billion industry – the wellness industry – with the potential to be as formidable as the food and health care industries. Fortunately, a significant percentage of the dollars currently being injected into the wellness industry will go in at the expense of the food and pharmaceutical industries. I predict a life-changing – life-saving -- shift in how and where Americans will spend their dollars, essentially shifting them from a sickness economy to a wellness economy.

Much of the wellness-industry growth can be attributed to the health-conscious baby boomer generation of more than 76 million people born between 1946 and 1964. People in this group spent the first forty years of their lives compromising their health in favor of earning money, and now they're willing to spend the remainder of their lives allocating any amount of money to restore their health, slow the effects of aging, and improve their quality of life.

Those who understand this trend and choose to take advantage of the explosive opportunity it creates will be able to eliminate one of America's other major problems. Most Americans live month-to-month, most save less than 2% of their after-tax income, and government statistics show that 87% of Americans will retire into poverty. Since embarking on my journey into the world of health care versus sick care, I've discovered a devastating problem -- too many people believe they can't afford to take a proactive approach to managing their health.

Statistically speaking, the majority of Americans spend everything they earn in order to just make ends meet, with little to nothing left over for such "luxuries" as health maintenance and prevention. Buying organic foods or nutritional supplements over the long term is just not in the cards for most families. In all too many cases, Americans end up deciding between buying food or purchasing their medications – and in these extreme cases wellness and preventive measures are rarely considered.

When you're sick and forced to spend money on never-ending medical bills and medications, it can be extremely financially challenging. Large percentages of bankruptcies in this country are the result of a major health crisis within the family. And if you have an insurance plan that is governed by a Health Maintenance Organization (HMO), you may find that your hard-earned dollars spent on monthly insurance premiums may not even be providing adequate coverage.

Managed care corporations siphon off enormous sums of money from medical care in order to reward CEO's, managers, and shareholders. If an HMO is in control, doctors are financially restricted from making independent decisions regarding appropriate patient care. It all comes down to cost containment in order to fund these corporate enterprises. So many people are incredibly frustrated by the lack of care provided by their HMO.

One of my wife's patients mailed her the following joke:

12 Signs You've Joined a Cheap HMO!

1. *Staff physicians include Dr. Who, Dr. Kevorkian, and Dr. Demento.*

2. *Tongue depressors taste faintly of Fudgesicle.*

3. *Annual breast exam conducted at Hooters.*

4. *With your last HMO, your birth control pills didn't come in different colors with little "M's" on them.*

5. *Your "primary care physician" is wearing the pants you gave to Goodwill last month.*

6. *Directions to your doctor's office include, "Take a left when you enter the trailer park."*

7. *Your kidney transplant surgery is held up while your surgeon awaits his arraignment for grave robbing.*

8. *The only expense covered 100% is embalming.*

9. *The only proctologist in the plan is "Gus" from Roto-Rooter.*

10. *The only item listed under covered Preventive Care is "an apple a day."*

11. *"Patient responsible for 200% of out-of-network charges" isn't a typo.*

12. *You ask for Viagra. You get a Popsicle stick and duct tape.*

If we're going to make a positive impact against America's health crisis, we must commit to providing grass roots education and showing people a better alternative. We must teach them to take some of the dollars they're currently spending on unhealthy food, expensive insurance plans, and unnecessary pharmaceuticals and reallocate those dollars to a program of optimal health and wellness. Embracing wellness and reducing sickness can provide people an opportunity to free up discretionary income, creating additional financial security for themselves and their families. If you embrace the wellness concept and are able to improve your health on any level, just think about the possibilities. Consider the following examples:

- A 55-year-old woman loses 80 pounds on a wellness program and saves $300.00 a month because she no longer requires expensive medications for high blood pressure, elevated cholesterol, and type II diabetes. She is no longer missing work and is more productive while on the job. She's given a raise and is now more financially secure.

- A 35-year-old woman starts a wellness program that eliminates her chronic back pain. She's able to come off disability and resume a job that she truly enjoyed. She no longer spends $200.00 a month on pain medications and she uses the extra money to join a gym.

- A 60 year-old man starts a wellness program that helps him quit smoking and drinking alcohol. He's saving over $400.00 a month and no longer misses work. He eliminates coffee and junk food from his diet and uses all of his extra savings to pay off credit card debt.

- The mother of an 11 year-old boy starts him on a nutritional program because he has severe focus issues and has been missing a lot of school due to behavioral problems. While on this wellness program her son begins sleeping better, starts paying attention in school, and joins two sports teams. The mom no longer misses work now that her son regularly attends school, and she saves over $100 a month by eliminating ADD medication, fast food, candy, and soda from their budget.

- A 28-year-old man loses 200 pounds on a wellness program and saves over $800.00 a month by eliminating unnecessary pharmaceuticals, fast food, coffee, and soda. He's eating smaller, healthier meals and cooks for himself instead of going out to restaurants. He's in demand as a guest speaker at high schools, where he educates young adults on ways to embrace healthy approaches for weight management.

> *"A penny saved is a penny earned"*
>
> *-- Benjamin Franklin*

Real-life examples of renewed health and vitality are abundant when healthy lifestyles are embraced. Inspirational stories of improved health, vitality and quality of life can be found in a book entitled *"Chicken Soup for the Healthy Soul "*. This book was the work of world-renowned author Jack Canfield, co-author of the famous Chicken Soup series of books. Individuals featured in this book took charge of their health by cleansing and replenishing their bodies with a nutritional technology from Isagenix International of Chandler, Arizona. Although it's impossible to quantify precisely, I think it's safe to assume that the collective health care cost savings incurred through the improved health of the people featured in this book are enormous.

You should never put a price on your health, especially when proactively addressing it could save you precious time and money and -- most important – could enhance or even save your life. All of society can benefit from a healthier population that the wellness industry can provide. And finding a nutritional company and getting on a healthy regimen doesn't have to put a dent in your pocket book. Some of the best nutritional companies in the world have figured out a way to formulate their products so they can be consumed in place of a daily meal. This is one sure-fire way of shifting dollars from the food industry to the wellness industry. It also effectively addresses the financial concern that the average American has when it comes to adding the cost of preventive health care and nutritional supplementation to an already tight budget.

Additionally, there are some formidable nutritional companies that offer incremental product discounts, cash bonuses and other financial incentives to their customers in exchange for endorsing their company's products through word-of-mouth. By using their customers' endorsement as a powerful form of advertising and marketing, these companies have figured out that they can circumvent reinvesting the typical 50% to 70% of their revenue dollars back into traditional marketing and advertising expenses. Reducing or eliminating conventional marketing and advertising expenses leaves them with surplus dollars that are then used to pay out bonuses, create financial incentives and justify incremental product discounts.

This is a very creative approach to enticing happy, healthy consumers to share their testimonials and endorse the products. This popular business model essentially places the role of marketing and advertising in the hands of the consumers. These companies understand that word-of-mouth is the ultimate marketing tool, because one enthusiastic testimonial will excite a multitude of new consumers. Now, as these new customers begin shifting their dollars into the wellness industry, this industry continues to expand and more dollars become available to be placed into the hands of the consumers.

Remember, these dollars are derived from two sources: savings through better health and higher discounts, and earnings through referral bonuses. Wouldn't it be nice to get bigger discounts on your products or maybe even get them for free by doing something you do almost every day of your life? Sharing your personal opinion about an experience you had with a product or service and encouraging others to experience it for themselves. This is a wonderful way to be part of a growing, flourishing wellness economy and reap some of the financial rewards this multi-billion-dollar industry has to offer.

When we introduce wellness products to our friends, family members, and even strangers, we're doing something much more powerful than providing a "product." We're empowering others to take control of their quality of life as they travel on the road to better health. Entrepreneurs and economists are all aware of this lucrative trend, and we all have an equal opportunity to ride this wave.

There is no better time than now to get out of the sickness industry and align yourself with the wellness industry. Make a decision to embrace the part of this industry that best fits your needs, goals, and lifestyle. Initiate a proactive attitude when it comes to your health and overall quality of life, and remember that the mind is like a parachute and works much better when open.

The wellness industry is poised for tremendous growth for many years to come. When you experience a positive change in your life, get out there and share your results with anyone who will listen -- you never know whose life you can positively affect. The countless rewards provided by the wellness industry are priceless -- no if's and's or but's about it!

About the Author

Dr. Becky Natrajan is a board certified Gastrointestinal Specialist (Board Certified by the American Board of Internal Medcine). After completeing her Internal Medicine training at Hahnemann Hospital in Philadelphia, Pennsylvania, she fulfilled her Gastroenterology training at the University Medical Center of Tucson, Arizona. For 12 years she has operated a thriving GI practice in Tucson. As a member of the American Society of Bariatric Physicians and an advocate of alternative health approaches, she has successfully guided many of her patients in achieving safe and effective weight loss and enhanced quality of life. Becky and her husband Dan Maes, whom she met through the nutrition industry, have dedicated their lives to educating others on the importance of taking control of their health and achieving optimal quality of life. Becky's son Kathan is 10 years old and Dan's children include Ally age 6, Devin age 9 and Hailey age 16.